I

Zoella

Written by Kate Hamilton

Edited by Nicola Baxter
Design by Zoe Bradley
Cover illustrations by Lauren Farnsworth

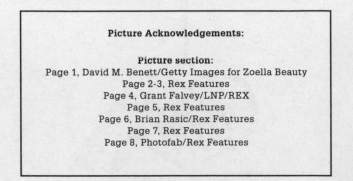

Picture Acknowledgements:

Picture section:
Page 1, David M. Benett/Getty Images for Zoella Beauty
Page 2-3, Rex Features
Page 4, Grant Falvey/LNP/REX
Page 5, Rex Features
Page 6, Brian Rasic/Rex Features
Page 7, Rex Features
Page 8, Photofab/Rex Features

First published in Great Britain in 2015 by Buster Books,
an imprint of Michael O'Mara Books Limited, 9 Lion Yard, Tremadoc Road,
London SW4 7NQ

W www.busterbooks.co.uk f Buster Children's Books 🐦 @BusterBooks

Text copyright © Buster Books 2015

Artwork adapted from www.shutterstock.com

A CIP catalogue record for this book is available from the British Library.

ISBN: 978-1-78055-383-2

**PLEASE NOTE: This book is not affiliated with or endorsed by Zoella or any of
her publishers or licensees.**

10 9 8 7 6 5 4 3 2

Printed and bound in July 2015 by CPI Group (UK) Ltd, 108 Beddington Lane,
Croydon, CR0 4YY, United Kingdom.

Papers used by Buster Books are natural, recyclable products made from wood
grown in sustainable forests. The manufacturing processes conform to the
environmental regulations of the country of origin.

I

Zoella

Buster Books

Contents

About this book

She's the girl with the infectious giggle and impossibly perfect hair who has gone from blogging as a hobby to a must-read blogging and vlogging worldwide sensation.

But, although she is internationally famous, she's still, as she says herself, just a normal girl, and that's what you love about her.

You may be a Zoella fan to follow her beauty tips or her shopping hauls, or maybe you like to know what's new in her relationships with other vloggers, especially her boyfriend Alfie Deyes. Perhaps you'd like to have a go at blogging and vlogging yourself, and Zoe is the perfect role model.

This fun book is full of quizzes and facts about your fave girl online, and there are plenty of tips about how to become an internet star yourself.

Grab a pen and follow the instructions at the top of each page – you'll find all of the answers at the back of the book. What are you waiting for? As Zoe would say, 'Be happy! Have fun!'

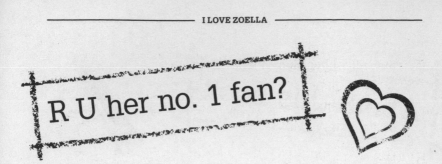

R U her no. 1 fan?

THINK YOU KNOW A LOT ABOUT ZOE? WELL NOW'S YOUR CHANCE TO PROVE IT BY ANSWERING THE MULTIPLE-CHOICE QUESTIONS BELOW. CHECK YOUR FAN FACTS ON **PAGE 91**.

1. What job did Zoe have when she created her blog 'Zoella' in 2009?

   a. Shop assistant

   b. Internship at an interior design company

   c. Trainee beautician

2. Zoe once made a video that she is too embarrassed to put online of her on Louise's back with blankets over their heads pretending to be ...

   a. Ghosts

   b. Moths

   c. A camel

3. She once embarrassed herself by seeing a famous singer in a shop and then playing her album out loud to her friend on her phone. But who was it?

   a. Björk

   b. Meghan Trainor

   c. Paloma Faith

4. She called her blog 'Zoella' after her ...
   a. Pet's name
   b. Nickname
   c. Imaginary friend

5. How tall is Zoe?
   a. 5ft 3in
   b. 5ft 5in
   c. 5ft 4½ in

6. Her very first blog post, which she has since deleted, was about the cast of which TV show?
   a. *Friends*
   b. *Saved by the Bell*
   c. *Skins*

7. Zoe shares her birthday with ...
   a. Lady Gaga
   b. Justin Bieber
   c. Rihanna

8. She passed her driving test after how many attempts?
   a. One
   b. Two
   c. Three

9. What is the name of her grandad's Instagram account?
   a. Supergramp
   b. Grandadchippy
   c. Grandadrules

10. As a child she had ringlets in her hair that were ...
  a. Red
  b. Blonde
  c. Brown

11. What did Alfie say were the three most annoying things about Zoe?
  a. Loud gulping, being messy, sleeping on the sofa
  b. Having a weird laugh, bossiness, not listening
  c. Daydreaming, arguing, tidiness

12. What three things did Zoe say were the most annoying things about Alfie?
  a. Laziness, his laugh, long-winded stories
  b. Stubbornness, pinching her electrical gadgets, his short temper
  c. Eating in bed, taking too long in the bathroom, loud sneezes

13. One of her happiest places to visit is an old-fashioned theme park in ...
  a. The Isle of Wight
  b. The Maldives
  c. Brighton

14. Zoe bought flight tickets for Alfie's birthday in 2014 for them to go to ...
  a. Paris
  b. Rome
  c. New York

Beauty and shopping

ZOE 'ROAD TESTS' LOADS OF BEAUTY PRODUCTS AND IS MAD ABOUT SHOPPING. HAVE A GO AT THIS FUN QUIZ ABOUT ZOE'S STYLE AND FAVE PRODUCTS BY FILLING IN THE BLANKS. THEN THERE'S ROOM TO ADD YOUR OWN STYLE-FILE TIPS. TURN TO **PAGE 91** TO CHECK YOUR ANSWERS ABOUT ZOE.

1. A guinea pig is pictured on the front of a cosmetic bag from Zoe's beauty range, but what is he wearing?

....

Design your own bag to add to Zoe's range below.

2. What does Zoe like to wear on days when she doesn't need to go out? ....
....

How about you? ....

3. Zoe says she gets frustrated shopping for sunglasses because her head is shaped like which vegetable?
....

We are all different shapes and sizes. Which accessories do you find it trickiest to shop for and why? ....
....

4. Zoe's own beauty range includes a fragranced body mist called 'Blissful ....'

If you were launching your own pampering perfume, what would you call it? ....

5. To add volume to her hair, Zoe always uses mousse at the roots. Does she prefer expensive or cheaper mousse?
....

What hair secret would you share if you were vlogging or blogging about your luscious locks?
....
....
....

6. When asked which feature she likes to play up most, did Zoe choose her lips or her eyes?

....

You can guess what your question will be! Which of your fabulous features do you most like to draw attention to?

....

7. In a Valentine's make-up tutorial, Zoe named a lipstick that was her 'favourite lipstick ever, ever, ever'. What was it?

....

Okay, so what is your favourite lipstick ever, ever, ever?

....

8. Zoe once shared that she owns a cushion in the shape of a biscuit! What kind of biscuit?

....

What's the quirkiest decoration in your bedroom?

....

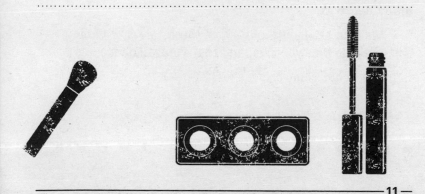

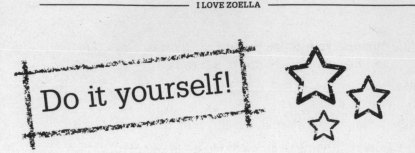

Do it yourself!

STARTING A BLOG OR VLOG MIGHT SOUND DAUNTING, BUT WHY NOT GIVE IT A TRY? ZOE HAS SOME GREAT ADVICE TO SHARE WITH YOU THAT WILL MAKE THINGS GO AS SMOOTHLY AS POSSIBLE.

If you enjoy it then viewers will too ...

> 'I think the main thing that really makes it work is that, if you're having fun, being yourself and filming something that you would watch yourself, it becomes contagious for other people to watch too.'

Zoe says one of the most important things to remember is to be yourself. She's just a normal girl, sharing her life through her vlog, and this is something her followers can really relate to.

> 'As long as you are putting in the effort and filming things that you love, and that your audience are interested in, you'll do well.'

Engage with your followers ...

> 'Your audience are what makes you, so you have to give as much back as you can.'

Vlogging or blogging is a great opportunity for you to share your own experiences and help others who might be going through a similar thing. In her vlog, Zoe offers general advice to her followers on lots of things from boys and dating to general issues that come with being young.

> 'You could say I'm like a kind of modern agony aunt.'

Remember to relax ...

> 'I used to be so nervous, but over time the camera becomes your friend. Be yourself, talk about things that you are passionate about and that you enjoy. And ask around — does anyone you know make videos?'

Zoe says that sometimes the success of her YouTube show can be stressful. When this happens, she takes some time to herself, away from the camera. You should never feel pressurised to post and if you want a break, take it.

> 'The great thing is that your audience know you're only human, and if you tell them you need a few days off filming, they'll be fine.'

When you are trying to decide a topic for your blog or vlog, start by thinking about what interests you. If you are really passionate about a subject and know a lot about it, your enthusiasm will come across in your posts.

'I chose to write about the things I liked, the things I'd purchased & other opinions on products in general.'

A good way to raise awareness of your new blog or vlog is to get involved in the online community and start following other bloggers. When Zoe first started her blog, she joined Twitter and became a part of the beauty community.

'I would read and comment on other blogs (personal comments not my blog link) and eventually more people would hop on over and join.'

When you first start your blog or vlog, it's important to remember it will take time to build up followers, so be patient. The most important thing is to get stuck in and have fun.

'I know it may be frustrating to those of you who have written a few posts and feel as though nobody is listening, but nobody was listening to me at one point either.'

Zoe says that you should make your blog or vlog for you and not worry what others might think:

'If you desperately want to make videos, and it's something you think you might enjoy, then who cares what anyone else thinks?'

Remember that you are in control. If you decide that you don't want to share your posts with lots of people, that's fine. The internet is so vast that if you don't link your blog or vlog anywhere it is unlikely people will just stumble upon it.

'You don't have to publish it to your personal social networking sites if you really don't want anyone finding out.'

Parents are you best friends ...

'If you are under the age of 16, make sure it's okay with your parents that you start making videos on YouTube.'

Learn as you go along. It will take time and patience to master your videos and become technically proficient. Zoe says she finds Google usually has the answers if something isn't working or she has a technical question.

'I'm not as tech savvy as some YouTubers, but I'm a lot better than my grandparents.'

Six things to remember for your web safety ...

1. Whenever you're about to post something online, pause and just imagine someone in authority, someone you respect, looking at it. If that feels uncomfortable, don't do it.

2. Never say where you live or give out your private email address or mobile number.

3. When posting pictures or videos of your home or home town, be sure that the location cannot be traced. Avoid place names.

4. To protect your blog from being hacked, use a complicated password.

5. Think of your future. Remember that anything you post becomes permanent in cyberspace and what you say and do now may one day cause you problems. Imagine a future employer, relative or close friend seeing it.

6. Do not arrange to meet anyone in person who you first 'meet' online. People may not be who you think they are or who they say they are.

Sweet tweets

ZOE LIKES TO STAY IN TOUCH WITH HER MILLIONS OF FOLLOWERS VIA TWITTER. HERE ARE A FEW OF HER SWEETEST MESSAGES TO YOU, HER BIGGEST FANS.

It makes me smile so much that so many of you find happiness in my random vlogs & videos!

....

It makes me so emosh that you are all so excited, happy & supportive of all the crazy opportunities I get. It's like having millions of BFFs

....

You guys are the best. Just a friendly Sunday night reminder

....

I would love to take the opportunity whilst I have internet for a further 8 minutes that I love you. Yes, you reading this <3

....

Bursting with pride at how strong and supportive the YouTube & Blogging community are <3

....

A day with Zoe

IMAGINE SPENDING A DREAM DAY WITH ZOE! FILL IN THE
BLANK SPACES IN THE STORY BELOW TO MAKE THE DAY
JUST THE WAY YOU'D LIKE IT. HAVE FUN!

You can hardly contain your excitement. An email has just
arrived informing you that you have won a competition.
Yes, won! But not just any competition. And not just any
old prize. You – and a friend – are actually going to (gulp!)
spend a day with Zoe Sugg!

And what better way to meet her than being whisked in a
chauffeur-driven limo right to her front door!

When the big day arrives, you and your friend ....
are so excited that your hearts are thumping and you can
barely speak as you climb into the swanky car. Luckily a
PR is there to escort you and see that all goes smoothly!

The car comes to a halt outside Zoe's house and the
chauffeur opens the door for you to step out. The PR
knocks on the door as you wait nervously. Your nerves are
forgotten the minute Zoe opens the door with a big smile

on her face and says, '..

....

....,

She's just as friendly in real life as on screen. You just have

to tell her, '..

....,'

Zoe welcomes you inside and at once you notice ....

....

Zoe asks if you would like a tour of the house. Of course

you would! She shows you into the front room and you see

....

The colours are mainly ....

and there are ....

As you look around, you particularly like the

.... and the ....

....

She then shows you her bedroom which you recognise from

the pictures in her 'Interiors Bedroom Snippets' blog. You

tell her how much you like ....

....

....

After that she shows you various other rooms and then her

spare bedroom where she does most of her vlogs.

You can't believe it when she tells you and your friend to

sit down in front of the camera to make your very own vlog

in Zoe's house! The camera is switched on and Zoe sits down between the pair of you and starts asking you about your life.

'What are your five favourite items of clothing?'

....

....

'Do you have a favourite perfume or brand of make-up?'

....

....

'What has been your biggest fashion disaster?'

....

....

'What is your favourite holiday destination and why?'

....

....

'Tell me your favourite joke?'...

....

....

All of you fall about laughing (even though you know the joke, Zoe has an infectious laugh). It's a lovely ending to a fun filming session. Then it's off to a restaurant for something to eat. Zoe gets into the limo with you and from the menu Zoe asks for ....

....

You choose ....,

and your friend goes for ....

After you have finished Zoe smiles and asks, 'Right, anyone up for a shopping haul?'

Shopping with the 'Queen of hauls' – it doesn't get much better than this! The PR smiles and tells your and your

friend that you both have prize money worth .... to spend on what you like!

Zoe takes you to some of her favourite shops. In

.... you buy ....

...., and

then you see a ....

that you just can't resist. Zoe holds up a ....

and says that it would be perfect for you and so you put

that in your shopping basket too. Onto the next shop,

................................, and here you bag a ....

.... and a nice

.... At the end

of the day, your shopping is packed into the boot of the limo and you say goodbye to Zoe. It's been a day you will never forget.

True or false?

THREE OF THESE FASCINATING FACTS ABOUT ZOE ARE TRUE BUT ONE IS A BIG FAT LIE. CAN YOU SPOT IT? TICK THE BOXES AND TURN TO **PAGE 91** TO SEE IF YOU'RE RIGHT.

1. Zoe is obsessed with hula-hooping.

☐ True   ☐ False

2. One of her favourite songs is 'Fields of Gold' by Eva Cassidy.

☐ True   ☐ False

3. Zoe's feet are so tiny that she buys her shoes from the children's section.

☐ True   ☐ False

4. When she was little she looked into the mirror to apply lipstick but got confused and daubed it on her reflection.

☐ True   ☐ False

Vlog planner

HERE ARE SOME THINGS TO THINK ABOUT WHEN PLANNING AND STARTING YOUR OWN VLOG. FILL IN YOUR ANSWERS, THEN GIVE IT A GO FOR REAL!

What do you like reading and watching on the internet?

....

....

What are your main interests or hobbies?

1. ....

2. ....

3. ....

Which of the above would you be most comfortable talking about in a vlog?

....

☆ ☆ ☆ ☆ ☆ ☆ ☆ ☆ ☆

Or perhaps you would like to focus on a new area altogether that you would like to learn about. Here's just a sample of possible subjects:

★ ★

Beauty	Gaming	Humour
Sport	Your life	Travel
Music	TV	Film
Dance	Décor	Animals

★ ★

Write your subject matter here:

....

....

What would the vlog involve?

....

....

....

The site would be called:

....

Would you do it on your own or with friends? If with others, name them here (and don't forget to talk to them about it!)

....

....

Where would you do the vlog from? (Bedroom? Living room? Outside? Garden shed?)

....

....

Viewers like to see what is around and behind you as you talk. Zoe has a fondness for fairy lights. What 'props' would you use?

....

....

How would you promote your vlog in order to get a large following?

....

....

Add extra thoughts and/or a script here:

....

....

....

....

....

....

....

....

....
....
....
....
....
....
....

Now have a vlog practice run. Grab a camera to film yourself and either use a script or fill in the 'Give it a try' section starting on **page 40**. You don't have to stick slavishly to a script though. Improvisation gives a natural feel and is more fun.

After you've done, play it back, see where you've gone wrong and what you can improve. Would you want to watch this vlog? Keep trying different approaches until you are happy.

If you feel your vlog still needs more work, come back to it another day. You may decide that you don't want to vlog publicly after all at the moment. That's okay. You can just do it for yourself and/or your friends. If you decide that it's not for you – you'd rather just watch your fave Zoella and other vlogs – that's absolutely fine too!

☆☆☆☆☆☆☆☆☆☆

Be Zoe's BFF!

COULD YOU REALLY BE ZOE'S BFF? WELL, BEST FRIENDS FOREVER NEED TO KNOW A LOT ABOUT EACH OTHER, DON'T THEY? SO HAVE A GO AT THIS FUN MULTIPLE-CHOICE QUIZ AND THEN CHECK YOUR SCORE ON **PAGE 91** TO SEE HOW YOU RATE AS A MATE.

1. You are planning a holiday with Zoe. Where would you go?
- **a.** Skiing in Switzerland
- **b.** Relaxing in the sun-kissed Maldives
- **c.** Trekking in the Australian outback

2. For a surprise you are going to book some tickets for you and Zoe to see a gig. There are lots of stars in town. Do you choose ...
- **a.** Miley Cyrus
- **b.** Justin Bieber
- **c.** One Direction

3. 'Let's go clothes shopping!' says Zoe, all excited. But where will she be heading?
- **a.** An exclusive shop with fab clothes at designer prices
- **b.** A fun shop with cheap, on-trend clothes
- **c.** A shop selling trendy outdoor and sports gear

4. You know that Zoe would love to be able to play an instrument, so for her birthday you are going to book her some music lessons. But for which instrument?

    a. Guitar

    b. Piano

    c. Flute

5. A cosy night in with Zoe, curled up on the sofa in front of the TV. But what would she most like to watch?

    a. *Breaking Bad*

    b. *Friends*

    c. *Game of Thrones*

6. Which of these male celebrities has Zoe had a crush on?

    a. Orlando Bloom

    b. Benedict Cumberbatch

    c. Channing Tatum

7. You arrive at a restaurant before Zoe and, as you are both in a rush, you decide to order for her. Do you choose ...

    a. Fish and chips

    b. Stir-fry noodles

    c. Pizza

8. Before meeting you, who does Zoe regard as her BFF?

    a. Tanya Burr

    b. Louise Pentland

    c. Marcus Butler

9. To make the most of a gloriously sunny day Zoe suggests that ...

  a. She takes the driving seat for a road trip along the coast, discovering new places

  b. You take the plunge with some Scuba diving to see exotic fish

  c. It's time to aim high with a thrilling helicopter ride

10. You're making chicken wraps for you and Zoe. In the fridge are three types of cheese to include. Which do you put in Zoe's wrap?

  a. Cheddar

  b. Mozzarella

  c. Halloumi

11. You know that Zoe was a big fan of Robin Williams, but which of the late funny man's films did she most enjoy?

  a. *Night at the Museum*

  b. *Flubber*

  c. *Hook*

12. You're on a long-haul flight with Zoe. What would she want in her hand-luggage?

  a. Chewing-gum

  b. Bubble-gum

  c. Jelly babies

Animal crackers

ZOE IS A BIG SOFTIE WHEN IT COMES TO ANIMALS AND
SHE LOVES HER PETS, BUT WHICH OF THIS LIST OF
STATEMENTS IS TRUE AND WHICH IS FALSE?
TURN TO **PAGE 92** TO FIND OUT IF YOU'RE RIGHT.

1. Zoe once kept several fish in a tank but she thinks one
of them 'murdered' all the others.

☐ True ☐ False

2. She named two of her goldfish Rosie and Jim.

☐ True ☐ False

3. Zoe's two guinea pigs are Pippin and Percy. Pippin is
the cleverest and can even recognise the sound of her
footsteps.

☐ True ☐ False

4. Zoe previously had two other guinea pigs named Milo
and Monty.

☐ True ☐ False

5. As a little girl she always wanted to own a chimpanzee.

☐ True ☐ False

6. Zoe had a bad experience with a rabbit when it scratched her arms as she tried to cuddle it.

☐ True ☐ False

7. Percy once got stuck behind the dishwasher.

☐ True ☐ False

8. Pippin once crept into Zoe's handbag and she didn't notice it until she got into her car.

☐ True ☐ False

9. Zoe's and Alfie's puppy is named Nula.

☐ True ☐ False

Chummy chatter

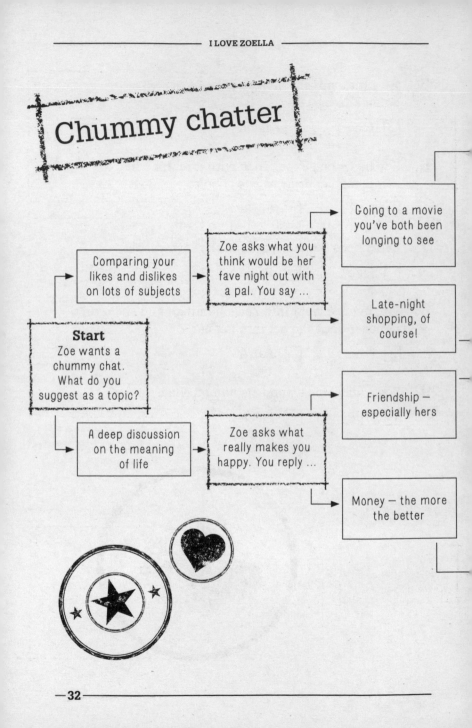

Start
Zoe wants a chummy chat. What do you suggest as a topic?

Comparing your likes and dislikes on lots of subjects

A deep discussion on the meaning of life

Zoe asks what you think would be her fave night out with a pal. You say …

Zoe asks what really makes you happy. You reply …

Going to a movie you've both been longing to see

Late-night shopping, of course!

Friendship — especially hers

Money — the more the better

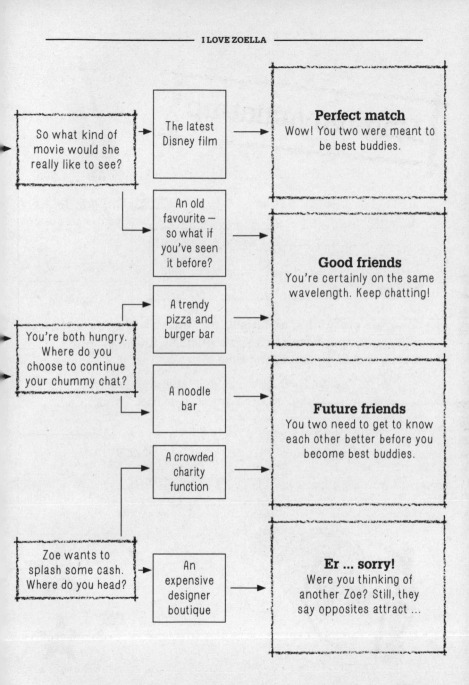

So what kind of movie would she really like to see?

The latest Disney film

Perfect match
Wow! You two were meant to be best buddies.

An old favourite — so what if you've seen it before?

Good friends
You're certainly on the same wavelength. Keep chatting!

A trendy pizza and burger bar

You're both hungry. Where do you choose to continue your chummy chat?

A noodle bar

Future friends
You two need to get to know each other better before you become best buddies.

A crowded charity function

Zoe wants to splash some cash. Where do you head?

An expensive designer boutique

Er ... sorry!
Were you thinking of another Zoe? Still, they say opposites attract ...

Magical make-up

GET THE LOOK BY SHARING SOME OF ZOE'S TIPS ABOUT BUYING AND APPLYING MAKE-UP, GATHERED FROM HER MOST POPULAR BLOGS AND VLOGS.

FAVES

Zoe loves everything about autumn, from hot chocolate to scarves, it's her favourite season, and she likes to change her nail polish to match the time of year:

> 'When the weather gets cooler I tend to move away from pastel nail shades and into deeper tones.'

> 'Some of the first beauty products I ever owned were from Barry M, does anyone remember Dazzle Dust?'

> 'When it comes to high end beauty, Estée Lauder is always a firm favourite.'

TOP TIPS

Zoe is a big fan of concealer, especially for dark circles under eyes. She's tried loads out there but one of her faves is Gosh Concealer No. 2. Zoe reckons:

'If you don't have this you're missing out.'

'ALWAYS moisturise ... especially under the eyes.'

Everyone gets spots, even Zoe, they're totally normal and she likes to collect them! But to help reduce spots and redness, she suggests using Origins Super Spot Remover:

'If you are looking for a product just to target spots once they've invaded, I would definitely suggest this'

PET PEEVES

Zoe hates when someone's face make-up doesn't match their neck:

'I just can't understand how some people get it SO wrong.'

'Horrible thin/thick eyebrows which have been drawn on (thin Sharpie or thick proper hardcore Sharpie haha).'

'Massive fake eyelashes in the form of feathers or something similar.'

OBSESSIONS

Zoe is a BIG lipstick fan, and even though she loves a bargain, lipsticks are her real weakness and she loves a high-end one.

'I purchased my first high-end lipstick when I was 20 on a shopping trip with my friend, and since then I haven't really stopped.'

RANDOM

'I am rubbish at applying false eyelashes.'

'90% of my holiday just consists of bare, makeup-free skin (with SPF of course).'

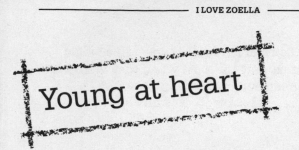

Young at heart

HER YOUTHFUL FACE AND FIGURE COMBINED WITH A CHILD-LIKE WONDER IS A MAJOR PART OF ZOE'S CHARM. AND ZOE HAS NEVER REALLY WANTED TO GROW UP. SHE LOVED HER CHILDHOOD AND TALKS A LOT ABOUT IT IN HER VLOGS, WHERE SHE HAS ALSO SHARED SOME CUTE VIDEO FOOTAGE OF HER EARLIER YEARS. SO THERE'S NO EXCUSE FOR YOU NOT TO BE ABLE TO ANSWER THESE QUESTIONS! CHECK HOW YOU DID ON **PAGE 92**.

1. Zoe would pretend that she couldn't swim in swimming classes so that she didn't have to go in the deep end and swim underwater. But why?

   a. So that she didn't get her hair wet

   b. She was afraid to go underwater

   c. She was just lazy

2. Zoe and her friend once sold posters and bunches of wild flowers to tourists in their village to buy what?

   a. Make-up

   b. Sweets

   c. Jewellery

3. Who did both Zoe and her brother Joe agree would 'wind up' their parents the most when they were little with their whining and crying?

   a. Both of them the same

   b. Joe

   c. Zoe

4. At what age did she have her first 'proper' kiss?

   a. 13

   b. 14

   c. 15

5. Which of Zoe's relations used large cardboard boxes to make playhouses and boats for her and her brother to play in?

   a. Dad

   b. Uncle

   c. Grandad

6. What insulting name did Zoe call Joe one Christmas which was captured on video and which she has shown on YouTube?

   a. Podge

   b. Pork

   c. Tubs

7. How much younger is Joe than Zoe?

   a. 18 months

   b. 9 months

   c. 24 months

8. At playgroup Zoe had a bust-up with her best friend Alex about playing with what?

   a. A scooter
   b. A trolley
   c. A teddy bear

9. What was the nickname she gave the Christmas hat that she liked to pull the fluff from as a toddler?

   a. Wobbly hat
   b. Bobbly hat
   c. Flopsy hat

10. When Joe received an electric guitar from his parents one Christmas, what song did Zoe start singing when she picked it up and started strumming?

   a. 'Jingle Bells'
   b. 'Tragedy'
   c. 'Smelly Cat'

11. The very first music album that Zoe owned was by which group?

   a. S Club 7
   b. Steps
   c. Spice Girls

12. What did Zoe say were her favourite sweets as a child?

   a. Milk bottles
   b. Pear drops
   c. Flying saucers

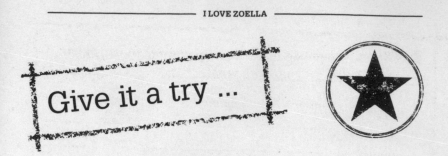

Give it a try ...

EVERYONE'S LIFE IS INTERESTING. IT JUST DEPENDS HOW YOU TELL IT. THAT'S THE KNACK OF BEING A POPULAR BLOGGER. HAVE A PRACTICE RUN HERE AND DEVELOP A WRITING STYLE THAT WILL INTEREST READERS IN A DAILY BLOG OF THE NEXT FIVE DAYS IN YOUR LIFE.

Day 1

A	X	T	B	M	U	V	S	G	H	A	L	F	I	E
W	Y	N	R	Q	U	Z	T	I	F	O	A	P	M	D
J	X	G	E	L	B	W	N	Z	I	E	T	S	K	P
N	L	S	R	A	I	Y	O	M	V	B	H	R	E	E
I	W	G	F	T	G	I	U	O	T	P	A	R	T	K
V	S	C	T	K	L	N	R	M	S	N	T	W	E	N
E	M	E	Z	Z	C	M	G	A	F	W	C	E	R	S
W	R	E	T	T	O	P	Y	R	R	A	H	Z	K	L
Z	J	P	M	U	P	E	R	C	Y	M	E	R	T	B
K	L	E	A	I	D	C	L	E	W	N	R	L	D	J
W	O	X	P	Z	E	W	B	L	X	P	J	F	E	A
M	U	P	T	W	X	B	U	Y	A	A	O	X	A	E
P	I	U	M	V	Y	O	U	T	U	B	E	Q	P	M
N	S	C	V	Y	U	M	W	A	S	Z	H	O	P	U
D	E	G	I	M	Z	E	Y	K	B	T	C	R	B	J

Timeline

SOME IMPORTANT WORDS AND DATES HAVE GONE MISSING FROM THIS TIMELINE OF ZOE'S LIFE. CAN YOU FILL IN THE GAPS FROM THE LIST ON **PAGE 48**? AFTERWARDS, TURN TO **PAGE 93** TO SEE HOW YOU DID.

1. Zoe's birthday is ....

2. She grew up in ....

3. Her father worked as a ....

4. Her mother worked as a ....

5. After leaving school, she started working in ....

....

6. She started her Zoella blog in ....

7. On 19 August 2013 she interviewed the boyband

....

8. On 3 November 2013 she was awarded Best British

Vlogger at the ....

9. She moved away from home in January 2014 to live in

.... by herself (plus two guinea pigs!)

10. She launched a range of ....

in September 2014.

11. She became Digital Ambassador for the charity

.... on 9 October 2014.

12. In October 2014, she moved into a big new house with

....

13. On 15 November 2014 she sang on the all-star charity

single 'Do They Know It's ....?'

14. Her debut novel, *Girl Online*, was first published on

....

15. On 11 February 2015 she took part in a charity special

of a popular British TV show: *The Great Comic Relief*

....

★ ★ ★ ★ ★ ★ ★ ★

Missing words

BBC Radio 1's Teen
Awards

February 2009

28 March 1990

Beautician

Lacock

Mind

Beauty products

One Direction

Interior design

Alfie Deyes

Brighton

Bake Off

Property developer

Christmas

25 November 2014

★ ★ ★ ★ ★ ★ ★ ★

Secrets, secrets ...

ZOE SHARES MUCH OF HER LIFE WITH HER FANS AROUND THE WORLD. BUT HOW WELL DO YOU REALLY KNOW HER? SEE IF YOU CAN SUSS OUT THE FACTS FROM THE FIBS AND FIND OUT HOW WELL YOU DODGED THE TRAPS ON **PAGE 94**.

1. Since getting very drunk when she was 18, Zoe has barely touched alcohol.

☐ True   ☐ False

2. The sun instantly makes her happy and the rain instantly gets her down.

☐ True   ☐ False

3. She has a phobia about jelly babies.

☐ True   ☐ False

4. If there's one item of clothing you will never catch Zoe wearing, it's UGG boots. They remind her of the children's TV characters, the Tweenies.

☐ True   ☐ False

5. Zoe once fell head first into a bin.

☐ True ☐ False

6. She has a little bit of a crush on TV presenter Phillip Schofield.

☐ True ☐ False

7. She bawled her eyes out watching the film *Marley and Me* at the cinema and all throughout the car journey home.

☐ True ☐ False

8. Zoe sometimes feels a little bit psychic and can almost predict what people are going to say.

☐ True ☐ False

9. Locks on doors worry her after she once found herself stuck in a public toilet and went into a panic until she managed to free herself.

☐ True ☐ False

10. When she was younger she wrote a fictional book about a girl who fancied her next-door neighbour and wanted to make him fall in love with her. Sadly, she printed it out but has no idea where it went and is unable to trace the original file.

☐ True ☐ False

11. She is terrified of deep sea. Thinking about looking down and knowing that it's such a long, long way to the sea bed gives her the shivers.

☐ True   ☐ False

12. Being a little superstitious, she once avoided walking under a ladder and stepped around it into the road and was hit by a cyclist.

☐ True   ☐ False

Quirky questions

ZOE IS ASKED ALL SORTS OF ODD AND WEIRD QUESTIONS
BY HER FANS. IN THIS FUN QUIZ CAN YOU MATCH HER
ANSWERS TO THE QUESTIONS? BEWARE, THERE ARE
SOME FAKE QUESTIONS IN THERE TO MAKE IT TRICKIER!
TURN TO **PAGE 94** TO FIND OUT HOW YOU DID.

Zoe's Answers:

1. A winning lottery ticket, please!

2. I think I would be happy.

3. Three light bulbs ... I think.

4. Going to Waitrose with Gabby.

5. Yes I do.

6. I wish that I could hear what people thought.

Questions:

A. If you arrived home to find that Alfie had thrown out all your unhealthy foods and snacks, how would you react?

B. If you could have any super power, what would it be?

C. What would you like to have in your hands right now?

D. Out of the seven dwarfs, which one would you be?

E. What's one thing you find that helps the most when you are feeling upset?

F. Do you sometimes pee with the door open?

G. If a guinea pig has two cousins who like carrots subtracted by the mass of the sun, how much did I spend in Topshop?

H. Do you ever wonder if we should be living life in reverse?

Write your answers here:

1. .... 3. .... 5. ....

2. .... 4. .... 6. ....

True romance

JUST HOW CUTE IS THE ROMANCE BETWEEN ZOE AND HER FELLOW VLOGGER ALFIE? IT'S FOR YOU TO DECIDE. THE STATEMENTS BELOW CHART THEIR ROMANCE. FILL IN THE HEARTS UNDERNEATH FROM 1–5, DEPENDING ON HOW CUTE YOU THINK EACH ONE IS.

Cute-O-Meter

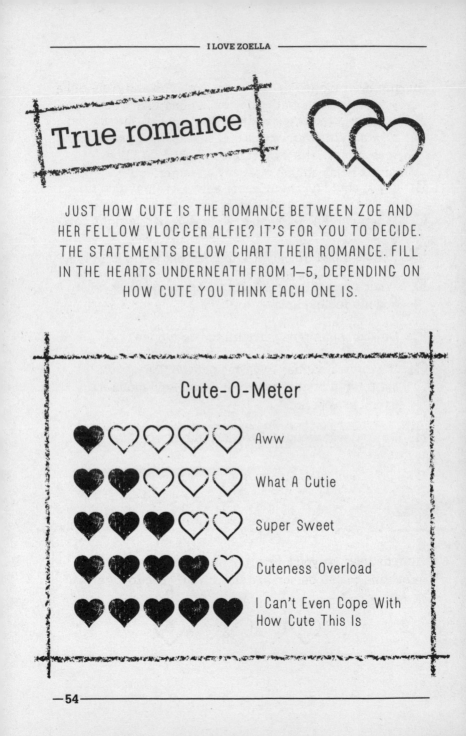

Aww

What A Cutie

Super Sweet

Cuteness Overload

I Can't Even Cope With How Cute This Is

Having been tagged to talk about love, Zoe and Alfie did a 'Love & Valentine's Day' video on her channel. They were just friends at the time but the signs were there!

'We waited until the perfect opportunity,' said Zoe. 'Valentine's Day couldn't get any more perfect.'

Zoe: 'I'd also just quickly like to point out we're not doing this tag because we're lovers.'

Alfie: 'Are we not?'

Zoe: 'We're not.'

Alfie puts his arm around Zoe and agrees that, 'Valentine's Day is just a normal day. It's alright that nobody loves you.'

Zoe: (sad face) 'Nobody loves me.'

Alfie to Zoe: 'Do you know that on my channel I only subscribe to one person and that's you?' Zoe touches her heart.

The pair also do a video on Alfie's Pointless Blog. It begins with him presenting her with a yellow rose and saying, 'Zoe, will you be my Valentine?' He then says to camera, 'Before you all start saying "Zalfie Zafie" ... we are not in a relationship. We wouldn't be cute together. We're not going to get married. None of that, guys. We are literally two friends making a video together.'

At the end of the video, Zoe looks to camera and tells the viewers that they should give the video the thumbs up to make Alfie feel better about being alone on Valentine's day.

Having announced they are an item later in the year, Zoe asks that her fans don't dwell on their relationship too much. The pair had been friends for a long time and every little thing they did was over analysed. This became very overwhelming when they actually started to like each other.

'Going through the stages of an early relationship is actually very daunting for me, now imagine if I was doing that in front of hundreds and thousands, if not millions of people.'

Alfie and Zoe said that they would wanted to keep their romantic relationship to themselves: 'We want to express that we will not be an "online couple"'

But even when her thoughts are about Alfie and their relationship, Zoe remembers to thank her fans: '... we couldn't be more grateful to have such amazing viewers with such great respect and morality.'

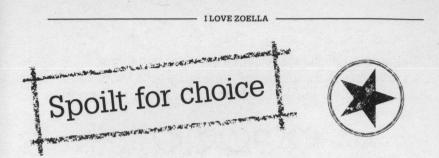

Spoilt for choice

SPENDING THE DAY WITH ZOE WOULD BE GREAT, RIGHT?
BUT IF YOU EVER DID GET THE CHANCE, WHAT WOULD BE
YOUR IDEAL THING TO DO TOGETHER? JUST FOR FUN (NO
POINTS AND NO PRIZES!) CHOOSE BETWEEN EACH OF THE
OPTIONS BELOW.

Would you rather ...

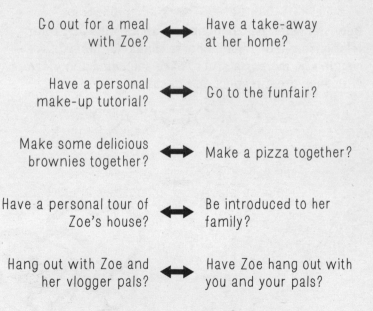

Go out for a meal with Zoe? ↔ Have a take-away at her home?

Have a personal make-up tutorial? ↔ Go to the funfair?

Make some delicious brownies together? ↔ Make a pizza together?

Have a personal tour of Zoe's house? ↔ Be introduced to her family?

Hang out with Zoe and her vlogger pals? ↔ Have Zoe hang out with you and your pals?

Go on a shopping haul with Zoe? ⟷ Interview her on camera?

Let Zoe take you to her fave holiday destination? ⟷ Take her to yours?

Have a Chummy Chatter? ⟷ Get a signed copy of her book?

Go roller-skating together? ⟷ Go bungee-jumping together?

Play 'Truth or Dare'? ⟷ Play Charades?

Watch a weepy movie together? ⟷ Watch a comedy together?

Help Zoe with some interior designing? ⟷ Help her test some beauty products?

Cuddle Zoe's guinea pigs? ⟷ Go for a drive together in her car?

Day of disaster

ZOE ONCE HAD A DISASTROUS DAY WHEN SHE AND HER
BOYFRIEND AT THE TIME WERE DRIVING BACK FROM HIS
PARENTS' HOUSE TO HER HOME — A FIVE-HOUR JOURNEY.
HERE'S WHAT HAPPENED ...

That morning she put on a new pair of trousers that her
boyfriend had bought her and noticed later there was a
massive split along the seam. She wore them anyway,
thinking she would be sitting in the car all the time.

After an hour's driving, her car started making odd
noises on the motorway and then juddered to a halt with
a bang. Luckily, Zoe managed to swerve on to the hard
shoulder. With smoke coming out of the engine, Zoe and
her boyfriend quickly got out and called the breakdown
services. She wasn't a member, so had to pay £140.

The police arrived and told the pair they had to stand
behind the barrier for safety. Zoe promptly stood on a red
ants' nest in her flip-flops and suffered bites to her feet!
And the hole in her trousers was by now gaping.

After being told that the car wasn't worth fixing, the
unlucky couple were dropped off at a Travelodge, along with
the car, only to find that there were no rooms!

They walked to a pub for something to eat and drink, where some scrap-metal dealers bought the remains of the car.

Left with a suitcase and a couple of bin bags full of their belongings, a taxi to the nearest train station and going back by rail to London seemed the best idea. Once in London they couldn't get all the way home because some of the tube lines were closed, so they had to get a taxi the rest of the way home. It cost a small fortune, and the driver was so manic that Zoe seriously felt she was going to die!

Even though Zoe didn't find it funny at the time, she laughs about it now.

Have you ever had a day of disaster that you laughed about afterwards? If so, recount it here:

....

....

....

....

....

....

....

....

....

That's life!

BEHIND THE SMILES AND THE SUCCESS, ZOE HAS THE INSECURITIES AND ANXIETIES THAT WE ALL HAVE. IN FACT, SHE HAS MORE ANXIETY AND PANIC ATTACKS THAN MOST. BUT SHE HASN'T LET THEM STOP HER. HERE SHE SHARES SOME OF HER VIEWS ON LIFE. BELOW EACH IS SPACE FOR YOU TO WRITE YOUR OWN THOUGHTS AND EXPERIENCES.

'Whenever I stop and think about all this, it's a bit overwhelming.'

What have you found overwhelming in your life? What do you think is the best way to cope with it?

....

....

....

....

'It's good for me to do things outside my comfort zone and push myself.'

Have you any examples when you have done this?

....

....

....

....

'I'm a total people pleaser.'

Do you sometimes try too hard to please everyone? How does this make you feel? Why do you think it means so much to you?

....

....

....

....

'I push myself to do more because it's just fear and if you let that win it's not helping anything.'

When did fear stop you from doing something that you later regretted?

....

....

....

....

'I am passionate about the need for everyone to feel ok to speak out ...'

When you have problems and anxieties, who are the people you would be most comfortable in talking to about them?

....

....

....

....

'So many people inspire me. I don't think I could pick just one. Even people in the street inspire me.'

Who has been the biggest inspiration in your life and why?

....

....

....

....

....

Zoe has learnt to ignore the negative attitudes of some people and to not let them get in the way of her doing the things she wants to do: 'I've learnt now that those who mind don't matter, and those that matter don't mind ...'

When has being brave and ignoring negative people been a rewarding experience?

....

....

....

....

'I think it's important to set goals and aims to give you something to look forward to and strive towards.'

Have you set yourself any goals or New Year's resolutions that you have managed to achieve?

....

....

....

....

....

Snap happy

THERE'S NO NEED TO SPLASH OUT ON EXPENSIVE
EQUIPMENT WHEN YOU START BLOGGING OR VLOGGING.
JUST USE WHATEVER YOU HAVE AND GET USED TO ALL IT
CAN DO FOR YOU. YOU CAN GET BETTER KIT GRADUALLY
AS YOU UNDERSTAND MORE ABOUT WHAT YOU NEED.
REMEMBER, ZOE WAS ALREADY INTERESTED IN DESIGN
AND PHOTOGRAPHY BEFORE SHE STARTED BLOGGING,
SO SHE HAD SOME TECHNICAL SKILLS AND LEARNT THE
REST AS SHE WENT ALONG.

How did you start filming your YouTube videos?

'I had a mirror in front of me and a digital camera on a
stack of books.'

Is it best just to start with simple basics?

'When I started, it was just a fun hobby. There wasn't really
an audience, so I had the chance to learn through trial and
error. My camera quality wasn't that good, and I used to
make my films in the evenings using a desk light. My first
bit of advice would be: try to use a half-decent camera if
you can — a standard digital camera works well — and try
to film in natural light from the window.'

What camera did you get next?

'... I decided that I liked the Canon EOS 600D (It's called something else internationally I think). I believe it is a fairly new model, but I am already in love with it'.

Your website looks great. How did you design your banner (the title image at the top of the site)?

'I used Photoshop to cut and stick different images together.'

What program do you use to edit your photos?

'I use Photoshop CS5 & iPhoto on a Mac.'

Up close and personal

TAKE THIS QUICK-FIRE TEST TO SEE HOW MUCH YOU
KNOW ABOUT ZOE'S LIFE, THEN CHECK YOUR SCORE ON
PAGE 94. READY ... STEADY ... GO!

1. What is the name of Zoe's debut novel?

....

2. What is the vlogging name of her brother Joe?

....

3. Who has a vlog called PointlessBlog?

....

4. What kind of dancing did Zoe do in primary school?

....

5. Which UK band's gig were she and Alfie at when
she had a panic attack and had to leave before they
played?

....

6. What one word name did Zoe's fans have for her romance with Alfie?

....

7. What three subjects did she get A Levels in?

....

8. What is Zoe's middle name?

....

9. Which vlog crew member and pal of Zoe's made a hutch for her guinea pigs?

....

10. What celebrity cookery TV special did she take part in for Comic Relief in 2015?

....

11. When Zoe interviewed One Direction for the movie *This Is Us,* which of her vlogger friends asked, via Skype, what super power they would most like to have?

....

12. What was Louis Tomlinson's reply to the above question?

....

13. During the same interview, Harry joked that he was going to get a tattoo of which female singer on his leg?

....

14. Zoe said that she shared the same dream as this 1D singer about going to school without any clothes on.

....

15. What is the name of the central character in Zoe's debut novel?

....

16. In the same novel what is the name of the guitar-strumming American boy she meets in New York?

....

17. What is the meaning behind the vlog name of Zoe's brother Joe?

....

18. When they were children, Zoe and Joe used to put cushions on the floor and jump over them to see if they could land on the sofa. Zoe once went for a long jump and hit her head on the wall, smashing what?

....

Beautiful bedroom

ZOE TAKES A KEEN INTEREST IN INTERIOR DESIGN. COULD YOUR ROOM DO WITH A MAKEOVER? WHY NOT USE ZOE'S APPROACH TO INSPIRE YOUR OWN STYLE? TAKE 'BEFORE' AND 'AFTER' PICTURES OF YOUR ROOM. GET A FRIEND TO HELP, IF YOU LIKE. MOST IMPORTANTLY, EXPRESS YOUR UNIQUE FABULOUSNESS!

Zoe has recently become 'obsessed with copper'. A small copper-wire laundry bin has been adapted by inserting a plastic bag so it can be used as a waste-paper bin. She has also bought some tumblers with a copper-coloured bottom and some nibble bowls in the same shade. Metallic accents add drama and shine.

Choose colours that express your personality. Zoe's favourite colours are pink and cream.

Another fun project that Zoe planned to make her place more 'homely' was to create a wall full of posters, framed pictures, photographs and postcards – including some with inspirational slogans, such as 'Logic will get you from A to B. Imagination will take you everywhere', which Zoe particularly likes. Yours could feature family, friends, hobbies or hunks!

'I absolutely adore shabby chic. I don't think it gets old or goes out of fashion.'

Some greenery adds life to a room and Zoe has bought several 'low maintenance' small succulent plants which she has put in white pots, to dot around the place. She also has plans to make a terrarium (a sealable glass container providing a self-contained environment for plants), which she thinks will look 'really cool'.

'The lighter and brighter everything is, the better.'

Bare floorboards, scatter cushions, fairy lights, white walls, cream and/or pink fabrics and furniture, yellow accessories, and heart shapes all contribute to the light and airy feel that she strives for.

As well as 'shabby chic', Zoe also has touches of retro and modern trends. Mix and match styles to create a unique look. It can be daunting when you move into a big empty space.

'I never knew what sort of style to go for but what I did know, is that when it came to my living room, I wanted it to feel cosy but have pops of colour'.

Getting an idea of what you want your room to look like is important before you start buying, making or painting. Zoe used the internet to research beforehand. There are loads of sites to inspire you too.

★ ★ ★ ★ ★ ★ ★ ★

Food for thought

ZOE LOVES HER FOOD — EVEN THOUGH SHE ADMITS THAT
SHE DOES EAT A LOT OF 'JUNK' AND WANTS A HEALTHIER
DIET. BUT SHE IS A LOVE IT/HATE IT KIND OF GIRL. FILL
IN THE GAPS BELOW WITH ONE OF THE THREE OPTIONS
AND FIND OUT IF YOU'RE RIGHT ON **PAGE 95**.

Zoe is addicted to ....
(bacon/cupcakes/custard)

'The smell of .... cooking makes me
gag/ want to throw up and don't even get me started
on what they taste like...'
(mushrooms/peas/sausages)

'I still eat potato ...., meant for kids don't
judge me, they taste damn good okay.'
(crisps/smiles/waffles)

'You wouldn't believe it but I'm not the biggest fan of
....,'
(chips/cookies/chocolate)

Zoe likes her dad's cooking a lot and sometimes thinks, 'Oh my goodness, I would do anything right now to have his ....'
(spaghetti bolognese/apple pie/mashed potato)

' .... ABSOLUTE YUCK!'
(Sun-dried tomatoes/Sun-dried raisins/Sun-dried beef)

'The only way that I'll ever eat .... is if they are so overcooked they are almost black.'
(chicken nuggets/fish fingers/pork chops)

If Zoe were to describe herself as a fruit it would be a
....
(tangerine/raspberry/pear)

Here are some foods that Zoe has strong feelings about. Put a tick next to one of the symbols to show whether you think she loves or hates the food.

Lemon cheesecake

Coffee

Pizza

Noodles   ☐   🙂   ☐   ☹

Fish   ☐   🙂   ☐   ☹

Garlic   ☐   🙂   ☐   ☹

Onions   ☐   🙂   ☐   ☹

BONUS QUESTIONS

What is Zoe's favourite American breakfast cereal?

....

What are the two additional things that Zoe likes to put in her hot chocolate?

....

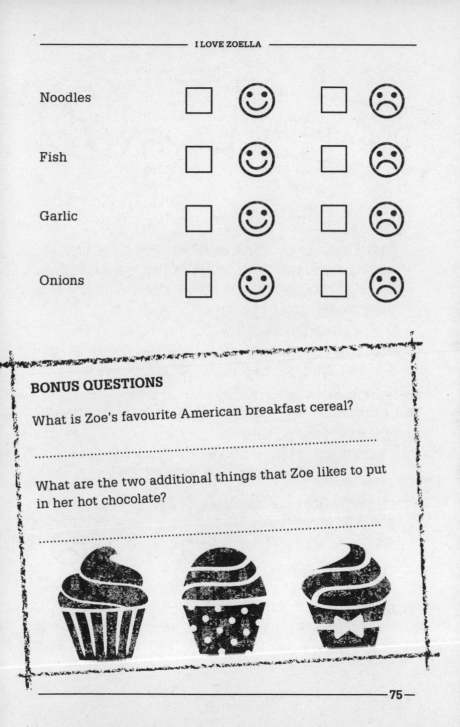

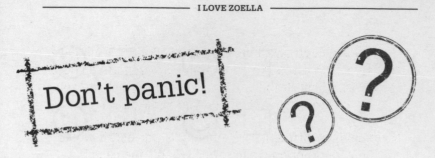

Don't panic!

ZOE HAS DOCUMENTED HOW SHE HAS MANAGED TO DEAL WITH INSENSITIVE COMMENTS ABOUT HER SIZE, ALONG WITH HER ANXIETY AND PANIC ATTACKS. SHARING HER CONCERNS WITH HER FOLLOWERS HAS HELPED, AS SHE NOW KNOWS THAT MANY OTHER PEOPLE GO THROUGH THE SAME EXPERIENCES. READ A SELECTION OF HER COMMENTS BELOW AND AT THE END THERE IS SPACE FOR YOU TO NOTE YOUR FEELINGS ABOUT ZOE'S WILLINGNESS TO SHARE HER CHALLENGES.

Body issues ...

'Whilst going through my teen stages of being a skinny bean pole, it had a serious effect on the way I saw myself and the way others saw me.'

'I hated having to go swimming as people would point and stare at me for being so skinny. I'd hate having to get undressed.'

'You always hear about larger people going through a tough time trying to lose weight, slim people can go through just as much of a tough time trying to put it on, but nobody ever really thinks of that.'

'If YOU are happy with the way you look, that's all that matters, and if you aren't, chances are you are doing something about it and working towards something you know you will make you happy.'

'Everybody is different, and nobody is perfect. It would be a very boring place if this wasn't the case.'

Coping with anxiety and panic attacks ...

'My panic attacks are a lot worse when I am stressed, or run-down, so I find it's really important to give myself a break.'

'I also tend to listen to relaxing music before I know I need to go somewhere where I may panic.'

'When I'm actually having a panic attack, I find the only things that really take the edge off, are going outside, walking away from the place I was and fanning myself.'

'Being anxious means you are more likely to find the negatives in any situation before the positives, and this becomes so draining. Not just for you, but for others around you.'

What do you think about what Zoe has said? Do you agree
with her? Which of Zoe's blogs have you found helpful in
your own life?

....

....

....

....

....

....

....

....

....

....

....

....

....

....

♥ ♥ ♥ ♥ ♥ ♥ ♥ ♥ ♥ ♥

....

....

....

....

....

....

....

....

....

....

....

....

....

....

....

Me and you

HOW WELL DO YOU KNOW YOUR BEST FRIEND? A VIDEO IN WHICH ZOE AND ALFIE QUIZZED EACH OTHER ON HOW WELL THEY KNEW EACH OTHER WAS A BIG HIT. ASK YOUR BFF THIS LIST OF QUESTIONS. YOU CAN LEAVE ANY OUT THAT YOU DON'T THINK ARE PARTICULARLY RELEVANT AND THERE ARE SOME BLANK SPACES TO ADD YOUR OWN.

My favourite TV programme is ....

My favourite movie is ....

My favourite colour is ....

My favourite book is ....

My favourite singer/band/musician is ....

My favourite actor is ....

My favourite actress is ....

My birthday is on ....

Name a food that I don't like ....

Name three songs I would like on my personal playlist

....

....

When or how did we first meet? ....

....

Who is the most famous person I have ever met? ....

....

Add your own questions in the spaces below.

....

....

....

....

....

Underline your answer in these multiple choice questions.

1. I prefer chocolate/crisps/nuts.

2. On holiday I like to sunbathe by the pool/explore nature/go sight-seeing.

3. Next time we spend the day together I can't wait to go shopping/to the cinema/to a restaurant.

Which of us is ...

... the untidiest?
You or Me

... the most organised?
You or Me

... the most punctual?
You or Me

... the funniest?
You or Me

... the loudest?
You or Me

... the most moody?
You or Me

... the biggest giggler?
You or Me

... the shyest?
You or Me

... the clumsiest?
You or Me

Did you agree? If there were things you didn't know about each other before, you do now!

Extra attraction

ZOE HAS BEEN AN EXTRA IN TWO HARRY POTTER FILMS AND THE TV PERIOD DRAMA SERIES *CRANFORD*. WHAT SHOW WOULD YOU LIKE TO BE PART OF? CHOOSE BETWEEN THE OPTIONS GIVEN (OR COME UP WITH YOUR OWN IDEAS) AND THEN ADD A FEW WORDS IN THE LINE BELOW EACH, DESCRIBING YOUR CHARACTER.

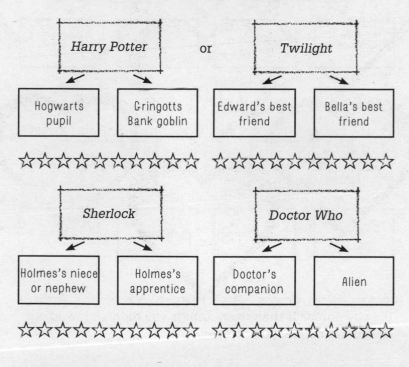

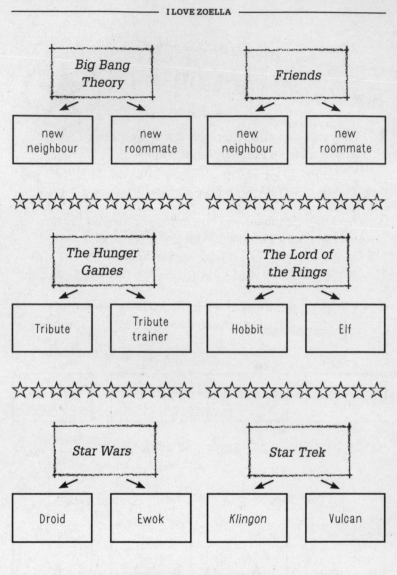

NOW SEE IF YOU ARE A ZOE FILM AND TV BUFF BY ANSWERING THESE QUESTIONS. THE ANSWERS ARE ON **PAGE 95**.

1. How old was she when she was an extra in *Harry Potter and the Philosopher's Stone*? ....

2. Which Hogwart's house was she in? ....

3. And which house was she in for her second Potter movie, *Harry Potter and the Chamber of Secrets*?

....

4. Which members of Zoe's family were also extras in the BBC period drama *Cranford*? (one point for each)

....

5. Which superhero character did she watch in a movie with *Harry Potter* stars Daniel Radcliffe, Rupert Grint and Emma Watson?

....

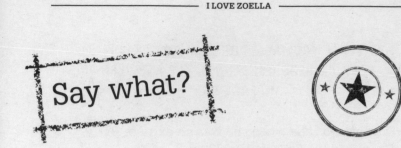

Say what?

WE ALL KNOW THAT ZOE TALKS A LOT OF SENSE AND TAKES THE TIME TO GIVE ADVICE AND GUIDANCE TO THOSE WHO WANT IT, BUT SOMETIMES HER BUBBLY PERSONALITY CAUSES WORDS TO SPILL OUT IN AN AMUSING AND SOMETIMES CONFUSING WAY. TAKE A LOOK AT THE EXAMPLES BELOW. JUST FOR FUN, GIVE EACH COMMENT A 'HILARIOUS' AND 'CONFUSED' RATING BY COLOURING IN THE STARS.

'When I'm old and wrinkly, I'll hope I can watch back at those clips of people screaming whilst I'm stood on a stage and remember it with smiles (possibly not my teeth mind you).'

HOW HILARIOUS   HOW CONFUSING

'I once said that Brazil was in Spain.'

HOW HILARIOUS   HOW CONFUSING

'My feet never smell. That's a fact.'

☆☆☆   ☆☆☆
HOW HILARIOUS   HOW CONFUSING

'Don't you just hate when you are around people you don't really know and you can't fully go for a sneeze? You can't fully commit into the sneeze so you kind of withhold your sneeze. And you kind of end up just going, "e-huur". It's like the worst.'

☆☆☆   ☆☆☆
HOW HILARIOUS   HOW CONFUSING

'Give this video a "pug up!"'

☆☆☆   ☆☆☆
HOW HILARIOUS   HOW CONFUSING

'Me and Gabby have very similar tastes. Everything that I love she has and everything that I ... she loves, I have ... everything I like she likes. Does that make sense?'

☆☆☆   ☆☆☆
HOW HILARIOUS   HOW CONFUSING

'I'm going to take my koalas off.'

☆☆☆
HOW HILARIOUS

☆☆☆
HOW CONFUSING

'Twenty five minutes doesn't seem like a long time unless you're cooking a pizza.'

☆☆☆
HOW HILARIOUS

☆☆☆
HOW CONFUSING

'Just burnt my tongue on a mange tout.'

☆☆☆
HOW HILARIOUS

☆☆☆
HOW CONFUSING

'So many of you have said it's snowing where you are! Where is the snow in Brighton? (My phone tried to autocorrect to B&Q haha)'

☆☆☆
HOW HILARIOUS

☆☆☆
HOW CONFUSING

Favourite things

ZOE IS THE TYPE OF GIRL WHO DOESN'T HIDE HER FEELINGS. WHEN SHE LIKES SOMETHING, SHE BEAMS FROM EAR TO EAR AND OFTEN REVERTS TO WHAT SHE CALLS HER 'LITTLE GIRL VOICE'. BUT IN THIS FUN MULTIPLE-CHOICE QUIZ, CAN YOU CHOOSE WHICH WOULD MAKE HER HAPPIEST? ANSWERS ARE ON **PAGE 95**.

1. Her favourite way to relax is ...
   a. ... take a shower
   b. ... take a bath
   c. ... take a sauna

2. The most enjoyable way in which she gets rid of things she no longer needs is to ...
   a. ... sell them
   b. ... have a car-boot sale
   c. ... take them to a charity shop

3. When asked what her favourite book was, she replied ...
   a. ... *Diary of a Wimpy Kid*
   b. ... Anne Frank's diary
   c. ... her brother's diary

4. Her favourite TV double-act is …
   a. … Itchy and Scratchy
   b. … Ant and Dec
   c. … Wallace and Gromit

5. She collects DVDs on …
   a. … knitting
   b. … musicals
   c. … Disney movies

6. One of her favourite drinks is …
   a. … Raspberry Ribena
   b. … Strawberry Lucozade
   c. … Cherry Cola

7. Her favourite number is …
   a. … 9
   b. … 7
   c. … 8

8. Her favourite song to sing in the shower is …
   a. … 'Let It Go'
   b. … 'Hakuna Matata'
   c. … 'Circle of Life'

All the answers

R U her no. 1 fan?
Pages 6–8

1. b	**5.** c	**9.** b	**13.** a
2. b	**6.** c	**10.** b	**14.** c
3. c	**7.** a	**11.** a	
4. b	**8.** c	**12.** b	

Beauty and shopping
Pages 9–11

1. Glasses
2. Comfy PJ bottoms or joggers
3. Pea
4. Mistful
5. Cheaper mousses work just as well, Zoe says.
6. Eyes
7. Rimmel Kate Moss 107
8. Custard cream

True or false?
Page 22

1. True **2.** True **3.** True **4.** False

Be Zoe's BFF!
Pages 27–29

1. b	**4.** b	**7.** c	**10.** c
2. c	**5.** b	**8.** b	**11.** c
3. b	**6.** a	**9.** a	**12.** a

Animal crackers
Pages 30–31

1. True	**4.** True	**7.** True
2. True	**5.** False	**8.** False
3. True	**6.** True	**9.** False

Young at heart
Pages 37–39

1. a	**5.** c	**9.** a
2. b	**6.** b	**10.** c
3. b	**7.** a	**11.** b
4. b	**8.** b	**12.** c

What's the word?
Pages 44–45

A	X	T	B	M	U	V	S	C	H	A	L	F	I	E
W	Y	N	R	Q	U	Z	T	I	F	O	A	P	M	D
J	X	C	E	L	B	W	N	Z	I	E	T	S	K	P
N	L	S	R	A	I	Y	O	M	V	B	H	R	E	E
I	W	G	F	T	G	I	U	C	T	P	A	R	T	K
V	S	C	J	K	L	N	R	M	S	N	T	W	E	N
E	M	E	Z	Z	C	M	G	A	F	W	C	E	R	S
W	R	E	T	T	O	P	Y	R	R	A	H	Z	K	L
Z	J	P	M	U	F	E	R	G	Y	M	E	R	T	B
K	L	E	A	I	D	C	L	E	W	N	R	L	D	J
W	O	X	P	Z	E	W	B	I	X	P	J	F	E	A
M	U	P	T	W	X	B	U	Y	A	A	O	X	A	E
P	L	U	M	V	Y	O	U	T	U	B	E	Q	P	M
N	S	C	V	Y	U	M	W	A	S	Z	H	O	P	U
D	L	G	I	M	Z	E	Y	K	B	T	C	R	B	J

Timeline
Pages 46–48

1. 28 March 1990
2. Lacock
3. Property developer
4. Beautician
5. Interior design
6. February 2009
7. One Direction
8. BBC Radio 1's Teen Awards
9. Brighton
10. Beauty products
11. Mind
12. Alfie Deyes
13. Christmas
14. 25 November 2014
15. *Bake Off*

Secrets, secrets ...
Pages 49–51

1. True
2. True
3. False
4. True
5. True
6. True
7. True
8. True
9. False
10. True
11. True
12. False

Quirky questions
Pages 52–53

1.	C	**3.**	G	**5.**	F
2.	D	**4.**	E	**6.**	B

Up close and personal
Pages 68–70

1. *Girl Online*
2. ThatcherJoe
3. Alfie Deyes
4. Country dancing and maypole dancing
5. One Direction
6. Zalfie
7. Art, Photography, Textiles
8. Elizabeth
9. Jim Chapman
10. *The Great Comic Relief Bake Off*
11. Marcus Butler
12. Time travel
13. Cher Lloyd
14. Louis Tomlinson
15. Penny
16. Noah
17. He is training to be a thatcher
18. A picture

Food for thought
Pages 73–75

Zoe says she's addicted to CUPCAKES but can't stand the smell or taste of MUSHROOMS. When it comes to potatoes, she still loves those POTATO SMILES that are usually served to kids but she's not a very great fan of CHIPS. She often longs for her dad's delicious MASHED POTATO but just can't bear the taste of SUN-DRIED TOMATOES. Zoe will only eat FISHFINGERS if they are cooked so thoroughly they are nearly black. When asked to choose a fruit that resembles her, she named a RASPBERRY, because it is small but has a big kick!

Zoe loves LEMON CHEESECAKE but she won't drink COFFEE. If you try to serve her NOODLES, FISH, GARLIC or ONIONS, she'll turn up her dainty nose, but a PIZZA will put the smile back on her face.

Zoe's favourite American breakfast cereal is called LUCKY CHARMS and she likes to add CREAM and MARSHMALLOWS to her hot chocolate.

Extra attraction
Pages 83–85

1. 10
2. Hufflepuff
3. Slytherin
4. Her mum, aunt and brother
5. Spider-Man

Favourite things
Pages 89–90

1. b
2. b
3. b
4. b
5. c
6. a
7. c
8. a